of home and family

everyday day

and welcome evening in

rejoice in the peaceful night

This is the Day the Lord Hath Made

Selected by
Jean Carpenter Welborn

The C. R. Gibson Company
Norwalk, Connecticut

Copyright © MCMLXXX by
The C. R. Gibson Company
Norwalk, Connecticut
All rights reserved
Printed in the United States of America
ISBN: 0-8378-2019-7

Let us rejoice
in the morning

This is the day which the Lord has made;
let us rejoice and be glad in it.

PS. 118:24

Be thankful for the beauty of the morning,
that you have eyes to see it and the
faculty to enjoy it. As the day advances,
forget not to be grateful over the small
joys as well as the large ones,—the new
flower, the book, the letter, the meeting
with friends, the kindly word. Be thankful
for knowledge, for the lessons that come
through mistakes and misfortune . . .

NORA HOLM

Every day is a fresh beginning.
Every day is the world made new.

SARAH CHAUNCEY WOOLSEY

The world stands out on either side
No wider than the heart is wide;
Above the world is stretched the sky,—
No higher than the soul is high.
The heart can push the sea and land
Farther away on either hand;
The soul can split the sky in two,
And let the face of God shine through.

EDNA ST. VINCENT MILLAY

. . . and in the morning you shall see the glory of the Lord, . . . The Lord gives you . . . in the morning bread to the full.

EX. 16:7,8

Life is full of beginnings. They occur every day and every hour to every person. Most beginnings are small and appear trivial and insignificant, but in reality they are the most important things in life.

JAMES ALLEN

Let us rejoice in the blessings of home and family

I'm glad our house is a little house,
    Not too tall nor too wide:
I'm glad the hovering butterflies
    Feel free to come inside.

Our little house is a friendly house,
    It is not shy or vain;
It gossips with the talking trees,
    And makes friends with the rain.

And quick leaves cast a shimmer of green
    Against our whited walls,
And in the phlox, the courteous bees
    Are paying duty calls.

CHRISTOPHER MORLEY

She opens her mouth with wisdom, and the teaching of kindness is on her tongue. She looks well to the ways of her household, and does not eat the bread of idleness. Her children rise up and call her blessed; her husband also, and he praises her.

PROV. 31:26-28

*How lovely is thy dwelling place . . . Even the
sparrow finds a home, and the swallow a nest
for herself, where she may lay her young.*

PS. 84:1,3

If I as mother sometimes err,
With moods as prickly as a burr,
With nerves on edge about to splinter,
Our family shows the gloom of winter.
But if I smile and give out hugs,
Admire Marty's box of bugs,
Take time with Bud to watch a bird,
Boost Linda's courage with a word,
And kiss their father without reason,
Then all our hearts know spring for season.

JEAN CARPENTER WELBORN

Love is the house it lives in; it is the cat
Curled on the hearth, the sunlight on the
      hedges;
But most of all, though it is all of that,
It is the love which spills around the edges
Because there is so much inside . . . the way
Tomorrow opens out of yesterday.

EDSEL FORD

For the gift of childhood and its family setting in our lives, we lift up grateful hearts. Though we cannot save them from trial or danger, we would, by example and encouragement, help them to find courage, wisdom, and love in our midst. We would learn from them as they experience the days of their years with us, and we shall welcome the day when they shall stand among us challenging us and offering a new companionship.

DONALD JOHNSTON

The dreams of childhood—its airy fables; its graceful, beautiful, humane, impossible adornments of the world beyond; so good to be believed in once, so good to be remembered when outgrown.

CHARLES DICKENS

To show a child what has once delighted you, to find the child's delight added to your own, so that there is now a double delight seen in the glow of trust and affection, this is happiness.

J. B. PRIESTLY

Let us rejoice
in the everyday day

Normal day, let me be aware of the
treasure you are. Let me learn from
you, love you, savor you, bless you
before you depart. Let me not pass
you by in quest of some rare and
perfect tomorrow.

MARY JEAN IRION

Like cold water to a thirsty soul,
so is good news from a far country.

PROV. 25:25

I read each letter through with
eager haste—as soon as it's re-
ceived; then re-read slowly—with
deep enjoyment, savoring the taste—
of piquant phrases, giving myself
wholly to all events described,
as being there. . . .

JANE MERCHANT

To live in love is to work in joy. The
time of business does not differ from
the time of prayer, and in the noise and
clatter of my kitchen, I possess God in
as great tranquility as if I were upon
my knees at the blessed sacrament.

BROTHER LAWRENCE

What is this life if, full of care,
We have no time to stand and stare.

W. H. DAVIES

Every man must take time daily for quiet
and meditation. Daily meditation alone
with God focuses the divine presence within
us and brings it to our consciousness. We
talk to God—that is prayer; God talks to
us—that is inspiration.

H. EMELIE CADY

Let us rejoice and welcome evening in

There is no place more delightful
than home.

CICERO

Now the table is amply set with dish
and glassware gleaming;
While from the stove the homemade stew
is magically steaming.
Gold biscuits in the oven rise, light
as a woman's humming.
Crisp salad greens curl in their bowl,
tender as footsteps coming.
The kitchen is a safe, snug place
wherein a mother sings,
Preparing a good meal with love—for
hearts are hungry things.

JOY BOWEN

The ornament of a house is the friends
who frequent it.

EMERSON

Stay is a charming word in a friend's
vocabulary.

AMOS BRONSON ALCOTT

Good talk has light in it, and dark;
        slow talk
Around a campfire with deep shadows,
        near;
A few hushed words exchanged as people
        walk
Up forest trails to watch old stars
        appear;
Awed speech of neighbors when a meteor
        scorches
A different pattern on a usual night;
And evening talk of families on long
        porches
Watching wide fields aglow with firefly
        light.

JANE MERCHANT

Let us rejoice in the peaceful night

Morning and noon are good,
but night is best—
Maker of stars!
　　Oh, give us back the night.

WINIFRED MARY LETTS

Now the day is over, Night is drawing
　　nigh,
Shadows of the evening Steal across
　　the sky.
Jesus, give the weary Calm and sweet
　　repose;
With thy tenderest blessing May mine
　　eyelids close.

SABINE BARING-GOULD

To see a world in a grain of sand
And a heaven in a wild flower,
Hold Infinity in the palm of your hand
And Eternity in an hour.

WILLIAM BLAKE

If there were dreams to sell,
What would you buy?
Some cost a passing bell;
Some a light sigh,
That shakes from Life's fresh crown
Only a roseleaf down.
If there were dreams to sell,
Merry and sad to tell,
And the crier rang the bell,
What would you buy?

T. L. BEDDOES

When you close your doors, and make
darkness within, remember never to
say that you are alone, for you are
not alone; nay God is within, and
your genius is within.

EPICTETUS

Lord, make me an instrument of Your peace
where there is hatred, let me sow love;
where there is injury, pardon; where there
is doubt, faith; where there is despair,
hope; where there is darkness, light; and
where there is sadness, joy.

FRANCIS OF ASSISI

Acknowledgments

The editor and the publisher have made every effort to trace the ownership of all copyrighted material and to secure permission from copyright holders of such material. In the event of any question arising as to the use of any material the publisher and editor, while expressing regret for inadvertent error, will be pleased to make the necessary corrections in future printings. Thanks are due to the following authors, publishers, publications and agents for permission to use the material indicated.

ABINGDON PRESS, for two excerpts from *Petals Of Light* by Jane Merchant. Copyright © 1960 assigned to Abingdon Press.

HOUGHTON MIFFLIN COMPANY, for an excerpt from *The Runner's Bible* by Nora S. Holm. Copyright © 1913, 1915 by Nora S. Holm, copyright © renewed 1941, 1943 by Paul H. Holm.

MARY JEAN IRION, for an excerpt from "Let Me Hold You While I May" from *Yes, World: A Mosaic Of Meditation* by Mary Jean Irion. Published by Richard W. Baron Publishing Company. Copyright © 1970 by Mary Jean Irion. Originally appeared in the *United Church Herald* (April 19, 1962). Copyright © 1962 by the Division of Publication of the United Church Board for Homeland Ministries.

DONALD JOHNSTON, for an excerpt by Donald Johnston from *Great Occasions* edited by Carl Seaburg. Copyright © 1968 by Beacon Press.

LIFE AND HEALTH MAGAZINE, for "Season Control" by Jean Carpenter Welborn as published in *Life And Health* magazine (June 6, 1964). Copyright © 1964 by *Life And Health* magazine.

J. B. LIPPINCOTT COMPANY, for an excerpt from *Chimneysmoke* by Christopher Morley. Copyright © 1921, copyright © renewed 1949 by Christopher Morley.

NORMA MILLAY (ELLIS), Literary Executor, for an excerpt from *Collected Poems* by Edna St. Vincent Millay. Published by Harper & Row. Copyright © 1917, 1945 by Edna St. Vincent Millay and Norma Millay Ellis.

NATIONAL COUNCIL OF THE CHURCHES OF CHRIST IN THE U.S.A., for Ps. 118:24; Ex. 16:7,8; Ps. 84:1,3; Prov. 31:26-28; Prov. 25:25; Ps. 4:8 from the *Revised Standard Version Of The Bible*. Copyright © 1946, 1952, copyright © 1971, 1973 by the National Council Of The Churches Of Christ In The U.S.A.

FLEMING H. REVELL COMPANY, for an excerpt from *The Practice Of The Presence Of God* by Brother Lawrence. Copyright © 1958 by Fleming H. Revell Company.

TILDEN FORD, for an excerpt from *Love Is The House It Lives In* by Edsel Ford. Copyright © 1965 by Edsel Ford.

UNITY BOOKS, for an excerpt from *Lessons In Truth* by H. Emilie Cady. Excerpt originally published by Unity School of Christianity.

WESLEYAN UNIVERSITY PRESS, for an excerpt from *The Complete Poems Of W. H. Davies* by W. H. Davies. Copyright © 1963 by Jonathan Cape Ltd. British Commonwealth rights granted by Jonathan Cape Ltd., Executors of the W. H. Davies Estate.

Designed by Betsy Beach
Set in Cartier

Photo Credits

Three Lions, Inc. — cover, pp. 10,15,16; Jay Johnson — pp. 2,3,22; Beth Welsh — p. 4; Robert Martin — p. 6; Steve Mack — p. 9; Four by Five, Inc. — p. 12; Peter Haynes — pp. 18,27; Bruce Ando — p. 21; Don Davenport — p. 24; Pat Powers — p. 29.

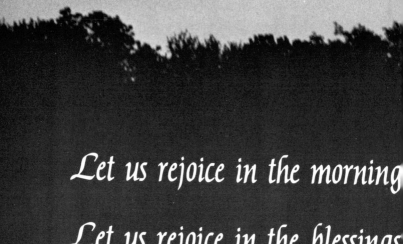

Let us rejoice in the morning

Let us rejoice in the blessings

Let us rejoice in the

Let us rejoice

Let us